JAMAICA BAY REFERENCE LIBRARY 02

JAMAICA BAY PLANT CATALOG

STRUCTURES OF COASTAL RESILIENCE
Jamaica Bay Team
Spitzer School of Architecture
The City College of New York

Catherine Seavitt Nordenson, editor
Associate Professor of Landscape Architecture

Kjirsten Alexander
Research Associate

Danae Alessi
Research Associate

Eli Sands
Research Assistant

JAMAICA BAY REFERENCE LIBRARY
REF 02 Jamaica Bay Plant Catalog

ISBN 978-1-942900-18-4

CONTACT
Catherine Seavitt Nordenson
cseavittnordenson@ccny.cuny.edu
www.structuresofcoastalresilience.org

SCR Jamaica Bay Team
The City College of New York
Spitzer School of Architecture
Program in Landscape Architecture, Room 2M24A
141 Convent Avenue New York, New York 10031

COVER
Laughing gull nesting area in Spartina patens at JoCo Marsh, 1990.
photo: Don Riepe

supported by

THE ROCKEFELLER FOUNDATION   SCR Structures of Coastal Resilience   CUNY The City University of New York   The City College of New York

Selected Plant Catalog

Plantings are carefully specified for distinct eco-zones
including Low Marsh, Marsh Transition, High Marsh,
Transition Slope, Dune, Grassland, Upland Perennial
and Ground Cover, Upland Shrub, Maritime Forest and
Ridgeline. Species with asterisks have been used in
restoration projects by the US Army Corps of Engineers
including the Gerritsen and Mill Creek ecosystem
restoration project, Norton Basin / Little Bay ecosystem
restoration project, and Elders Point East, Elders Point
West, and Yellow Bar Hassock marsh restorations. Other
species selections are drawn from model ecosystems such
as the Sunken Forest on Fire Island, New York, and from
the New York City Department of Parks and Recreation
Natural Resources Group *Native Species Planting
Guide for New York and Vicinity*.

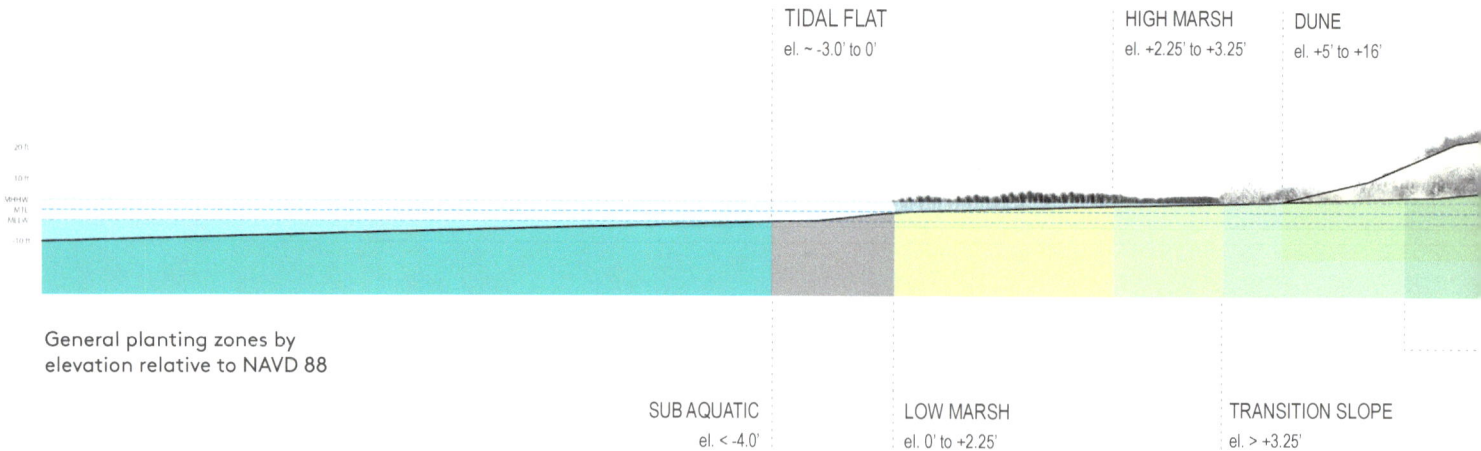

TIDAL FLAT
el. ~ -3.0' to 0'

HIGH MARSH
el. +2.25' to +3.25'

DUNE
el. +5' to +16'

General planting zones by
elevation relative to NAVD 88

SUB AQUATIC
el. < -4.0'

LOW MARSH
el. 0' to +2.25'

TRANSITION SLOPE
el. > +3.25'

7

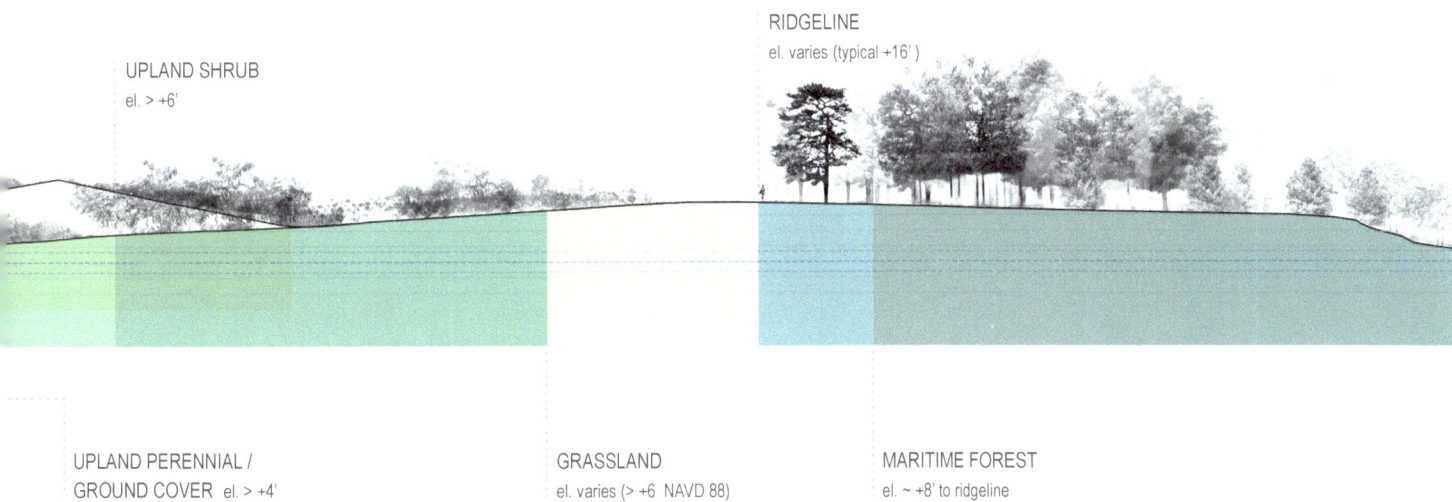

UPLAND SHRUB
el. > +6'

RIDGELINE
el. varies (typical +16')

UPLAND PERENNIAL /
GROUND COVER el. > +4'

GRASSLAND
el. varies (> +6 NAVD 88)

MARITIME FOREST
el. ~ +8' to ridgeline

Sub Aquatic

elevation range: approx. -4' to -10' NAVD 88
            varies depending on water clarity

Zostera marina   Eelgrass

Wetland: Low Salt Marsh

elevation range: 0' to +2.25' NAVD 88

Spartina alterniflora   Smooth Cordgrass* **

Wetland: High Salt Marsh

elevation range: +2.25' to +3.25' NAVD 88

Distichlis spicata   Spike Grass* **
Juncus gerardii   Black Grass / Saltmeadow Rush*
Spartina patens   Saltmeadow Cordgrass* **

Transition Slope

elevation range: > +3.25' NAVD 88

Agrostis alba   Redtop
Apocynum cannabinum   Indian Hemp*
Asclepias syriaca   Milkweed* **
Asclepias tuberosa   Butterfly Milkweed* **
Aster laevis   Smooth Aster*
Carex pensylvanica   Pennsylvania Sedge* **
Eupatorium fistulosum   Joe Pye Weed* **
Eupatorium hyssopifolium   Hyssop-Leaved Thoroughwort*
Eupatorium maculatum   Spotted Joe Pye Weed*
Lechea maritima   Beach Pinweed
Limonium trichogonum   Sea Lavender
Monarda fistulosa   Wild Bergamot* **
Panicum virgatum   Switchgrass* **
Rudbeckia hirta   Black-Eyed Susan* **
Salicornia subterminalis   Glasswort
Solidago sempervirens   Seaside Goldenrod* **
Vernonia noveboracensis   Ironweed* **

Dune

elevation range: approx. +5 to +16 NAVD 88

Ammophila breviligulata   American Beach Grass* **
Myrica pensylvanica   Bayberry* **
Prunus maritima   Beach Plum* **
Rosa carolina   Pasture Rose**
Solidago sempervirens   Seaside Goldenrod* **

* used in restoration projects by the US Army Corps of Engineers

** recommended native plant by Natural Resources Group

Grassland
elevation range: varies (> +6 NAVD 88)

Andropogon virginicus	Broomsedge Bluestem* **
Apocynum cannabinum	Indian Hemp*
Asclepias syriaca	Milkweed* **
Asclepias tuberosa	Butterfly Milkweed* **
Aster laevis	Smooth Aster*
Avena sativa	Common Oat*
Carex pensylvanica	Pennsylvania Sedge* **
Deschampsia flexuosa	Wavy Hairgrass*
Eupatorium fistulosum	Joe Pye Weed* **
Eupatorium hyssopifolium	Hyssop-Leaved Thoroughwort*
Eupatorim maculatum	Spotted Joe Pye Weed* **
Monarda fistulosa	Wild Bergamot* **
Panicum virgatum	Switchgrass* **
Rudbeckia hirta	Black-Eyed Susan* **
Schizachyrium scoparium	Little Bluestem* **
Solidago sempervirens	Seaside Goldenrod* **
Vernonia noveboracensis	Ironweed* **

Upland Shrub
elevation range: approx. > +6' NAVD 88

Amelanchier canadensis	Serviceberry* **
Aralia nudicaulis	Wild Sarsaparilla**
Arctostaphylos uva-ursi	Bearberry*
Myrica heterophylla	Swamp Bayberry
Myrica pensylvanica	Bayberry* **
Prunus maritima	Beach Plum* **
Rhus copallina	Winged Sumac* **
Rhus typhina	Staghorn Sumac**
Vaccinium corymbosum	High Bush Blueberry* **

Ridgeline
elevation range: varies, typical +12' to +17' NAVD 88

Pinus rigida	Pitch Pine* **

Upland Perennial / Ground Cover
elevation range: > +4' NAVD 88

Artemisia stelleriana	Silver Brocade
Baccharis halimifolia	Sea-myrtle**
Cakile edentula	American Searocket
Cirsium horridulum	Yellow Thistle
Hieracium venosum	Rattlesnake Weed
Hudsonia tomentosa	Sand Heather
Iva frutescens linnaeus	Marsh Elder*
Lathyrus japonicus	Sea Pea
Parthenocissus quinquefolia	Virginia Creeper
Smilacina stellata	Star-flowered Solomon's Seal
Toxicodendron radicans	Poison Ivy*

Maritime Forest
elevation range: ~ > +8' NAVD 88 to ridgeline

Acer rubrum	Red Maple**
Betula populifolia	Grey Birch* **
Celtis occidentalis	Hackberry* **
Ilex opaca	American Holly* **
Magnolia virginiana	Sweetbay Magnolia
Nyssa sylvatica	Black Tupelo**
Populus deltoides	Cottonwood*
Prunus serotina	Black Cherry* **
Quercus stellata	Post Oak
Quercus velutina	Black Oak* **
Salix pentandra	Bay Willow*
Sassafras albidum	Sassafras

SUB AQUATIC

elevation range: approx. -4' to -10' NAVD 88

Zostera marina   Eelgrass

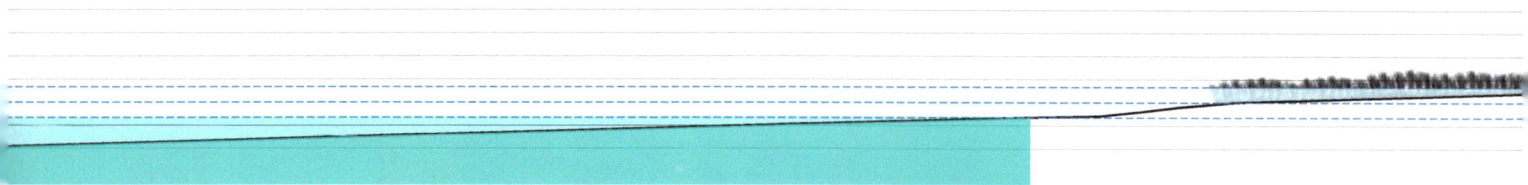

Zostera marina   Eelgrass

SUB AQUATIC
Elevation range: approx. -4' to -10' NAVD 88
                   varies depending on water clarity

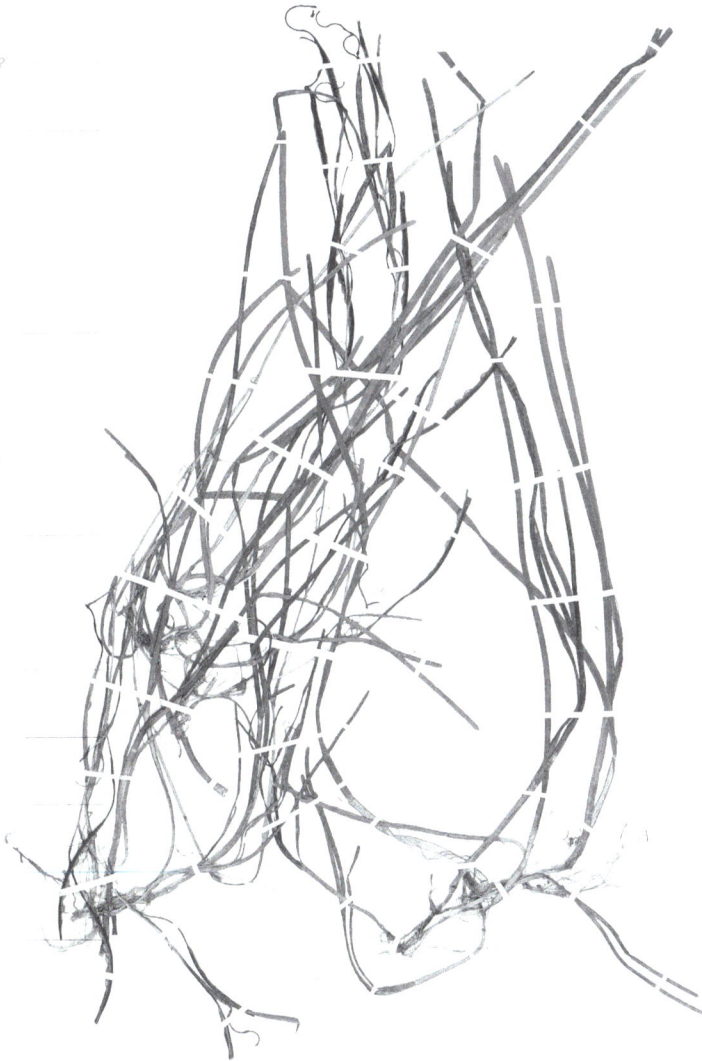

photo: Carol Cloen, DNR

scale: 1/3
specimen source Patuxent Wildlife Research Herbarium

WETLAND: LOW SALT MARSH
elevation range: 0' to +2.25' NAVD 88

Spartina alterniflora Saltmarsh Cordgrass* **

Spartina alterniflora   Saltmarsh Cordgrass* **

WETLAND: LOW SALT MARSH
Elevation range: 0 to +2.25 NAVD 88

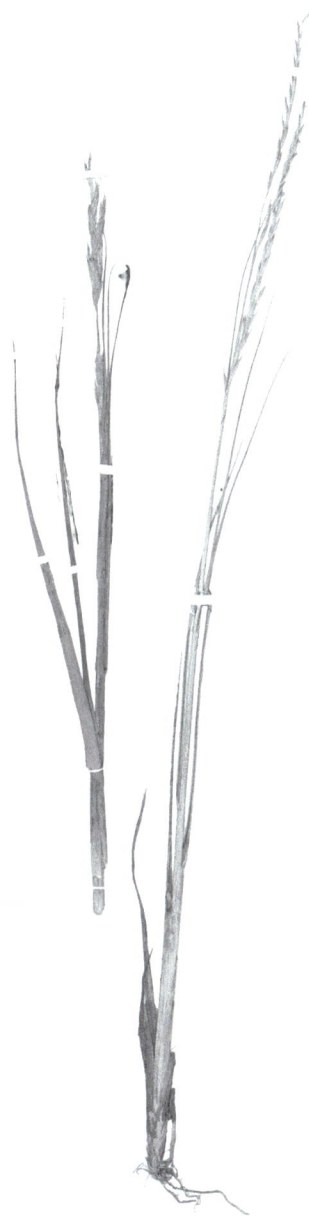

photo: Nelson DeBarros, USDA NRCS PLANTS

scale: 1/4
specimen sources: Herbarium of Iowa State College / Missouri Botanical Garden

WETLAND: HIGH SALT MARSH

elevation range: +2.25' to +3.25' NAVD 88

Distichlis spicata	Spike Grass* **
Juncus gerardii	Black Grass / Saltmeadow Rush*
Spartina patens	Saltmeadow Cordgrass* **

* used in restoration projects by the US Army Corps of Engineers

** recommended native plant by Natural Resources Group

Distichlis spicata Spike Grass* **

WETLAND: HIGH SALT MARSH
Elevation range: +2.25 to +3.25 NAVD 88

photo: Ron Vanderhoff, University of California, Irvine

12"

6"

scale: 1/3
specimen source: U.S. National Herbarium

18"

12"

6"

Juncus gerardii Loisel Black Grass*

WETLAND: HIGH SALT MARSH
Elevation range: +2.25 to +3.25 NAVD 88

photo: Biopix, JC Schou

scale: 1/3
specimen source: Lund University

Spartina patens Saltmeadow Cordgrass* **

WETLAND: HIGH SALT MARSH
Elevation range: +2.25 to +3.25 NAVD 88

scale: 1/3
specimen source Linnean Society of London Herbarium (LINN)

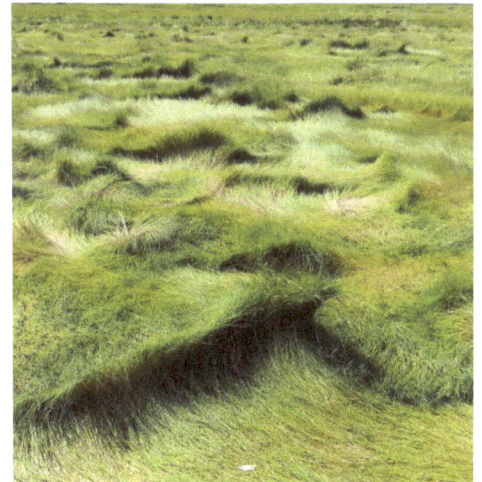

TRANSITION SLOPE
elevation range: > +3.25' NAVD 88

Agrostis alba	Redtop
Apocynum cannabinum	Indian Hemp*
Asclepias syriaca	Milkweed* **
Asclepias tuberosa	Butterfly Milkweed* **
Aster laevis	Smooth Aster*
Carex pensylvanica	Pennsylvania Sedge* **
Eupatorium fistulosum	Joe Pye Weed* **
Eupatorium hyssopifolium	Hyssop-Leaved Thoroughwort* **
Eupatorium maculatum	Spotted Joe Pye Weed* **
Lechea maritima	Beach Pinweed
Limonium trichogonum	Sea Lavender
Monarda fistulosa	Wild Bergamot* **
Panicum virgatum	Switchgrass* **
Rudbeckia hirta	Black-Eyed Susan* **
Salicornia subterminalis	Glasswort
Solidago sempervirens	Seaside Goldenrod* **
Vernonia noveboracensis	Ironweed* **

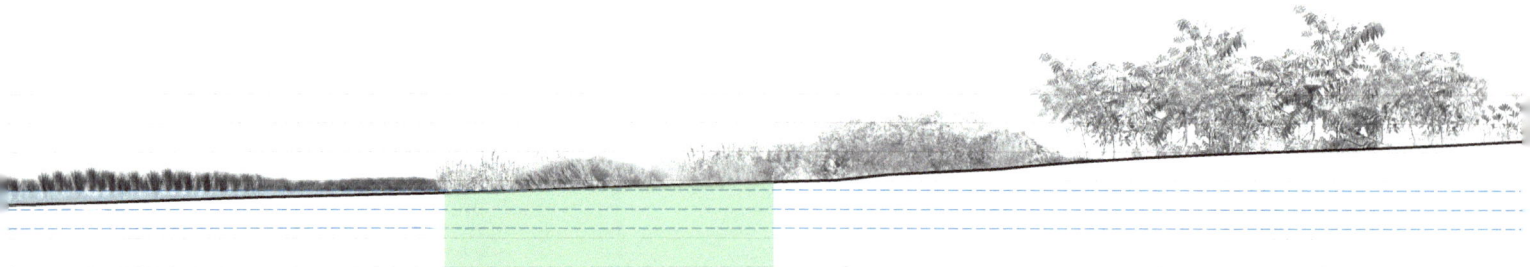

* used in restoration projects by the US Army Corps of Engineers

** recommended native plant by Natural Resources Group

12

6"

Agrostis alba Redtop

TRANSITION SLOPE
Elevation range: > +3.25 NAVD 88

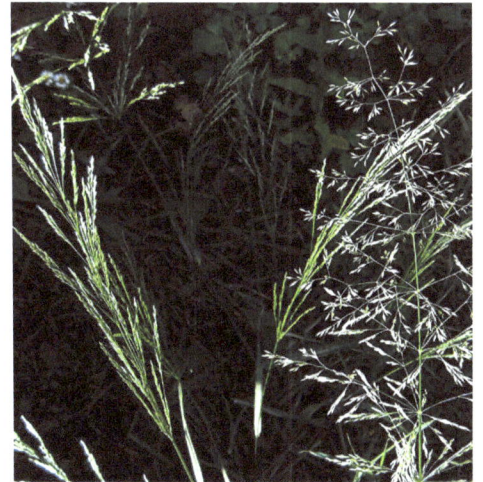

scale: 1/3
specimen source: Herbarium Universitatis Tartuensis

Apocynum cannabinum   Indian Hemp*

TRANSITION SLOPE / GRASSLAND
Elevation range: > +3.25 NAVD 88

photo: Russ Kleinman, Bill Norris, Kelly Kindscher

scale: 1/3
specimen source: United States National Herbarium, Smithsonian Institution

Asclepias syriaca Milkweed* **

TRANSITION SLOPE / GRASSLAND
Elevation range: > +3.25 NAVD 88

photo Stefan Lefnaer, Wikipedia

scale: 1/3
specimen sources Linnean Society of London Herbarium / New England Botanical Club

12"

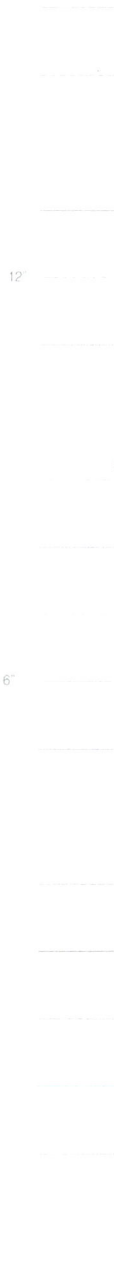

Asclepias tuberosa   Butterfly Milkweed* **

TRANSITION SLOPE / GRASSLAND
Elevation range: > +3.25 NAVD 88

6"

photo: Rus Kleinman. Karen Blisard

scale: 1/3
specimen source: Herbarium Desert Botanical Garden

12

6

Aster laevis   Smooth Aster*

TRANSITION SLOPE / GRASSLAND
Elevation range: > +3.25 NAVD 88

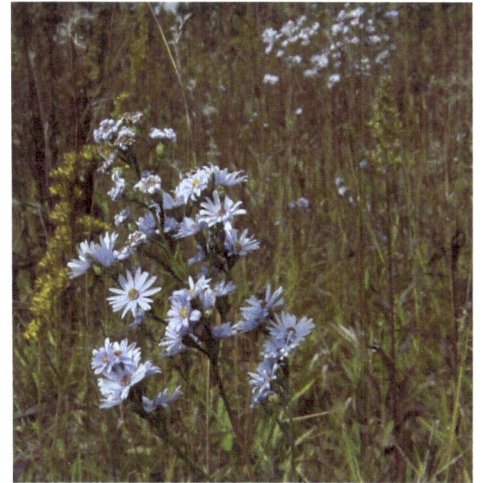

scale: 1/3
specimen source. Herbarium of the University of Washington

Carex pensylvanica Pennsylvania Sedge* **

TRANSITION SLOPE / GRASSLAND
Elevation range: > +3.25 NAVD 88

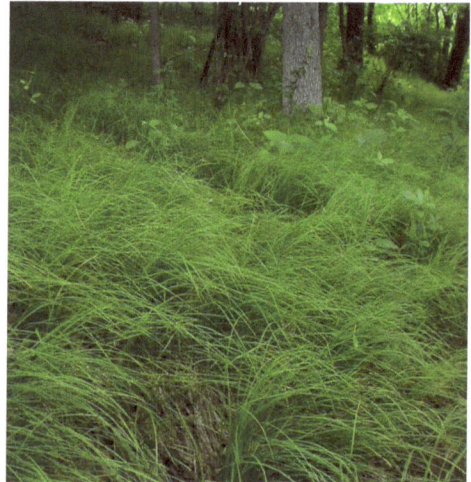

photo: nativeplant.com

scale: 1/3
specimen source: Academy of Natural Sciences. Philadelphia

Eupatorium fistulosum   Joe Pye Weed* **

TRANSITION SLOPE / GRASSLAND
Elevation range: > +3.25 NAVD 88

photo Centre de Jardin Brossard

scale: 1/3
specimen source Carnegie Museum of Natural History Herbarium

12"

6"

Eupatorium hyssopifolium   Hyssop-Leaved Thoroughwort* **

TRANSITION SLOPE / GRASSLAND
Elevation range: > +3.25 NAVD 88

photo: Larry Allain, USDA NRCS PLANTS

scale: 1/3
specimen source: Natural History Museum

Eutrochium maculatum   Spotted Joe Pye Weed* **

TRANSITION SLOPE / GRASSLAND
Elevation range: > +3.25 NAVD 88

photo: Cody Hough, Wikimedia Commons

scale: 1/3
specimen source: Academy of Natural Sciences

Lechea maritima   Beach Pinweed

TRANSITION SLOPE
Elevation range: > +3.25 NAVD 88

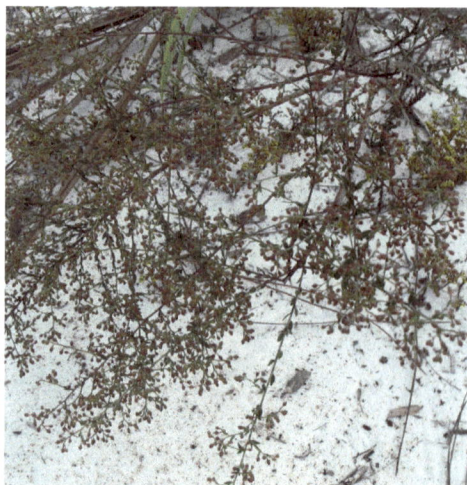

12'

6'

scale: 1/3
specimen source: New England Botanical Club

12

6

Limonium trichogonum   Sea Lavender

TRANSITION SLOPE
Elevation range: > +3.25 NAVD 88

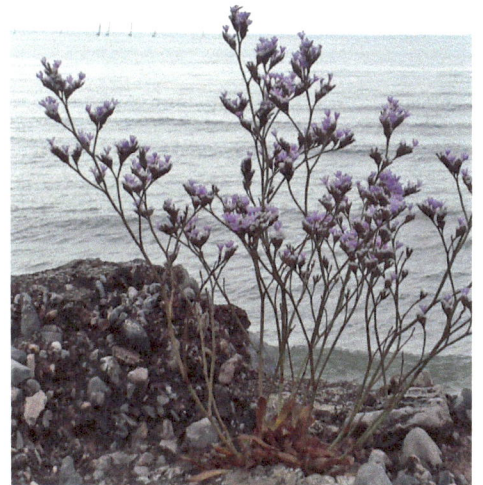

scale: 1/3
specimen source: U.S. National Herbarium

12"

Monarda fistulosa   Wild Bergamot* **

TRANSITION SLOPE / GRASSLAND
Elevation range: > +3.25 NAVD 88

6"

photo: Jacob Cline

scale: 1/3
specimen source: Herbarium of the University of West Alabama

Panicum virgatum   Switchgrass* **

TRANSITION SLOPE / GRASSLAND
Elevation range: > +3.25 NAVD 88

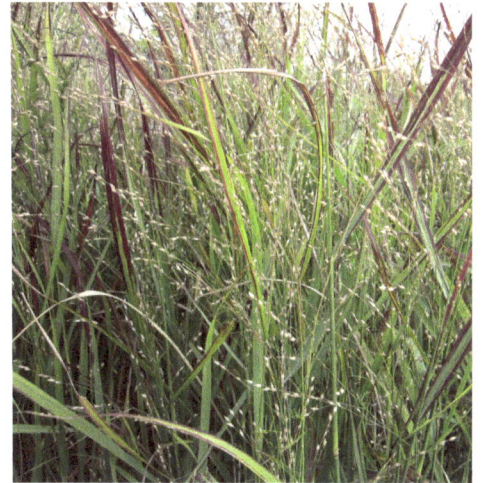

photo: Rose Kennedy Greenway

scale: 1/3
specimen source: U.S. National Herbarium, Smithsonian Institution

Rudbeckia hirta   Black-Eyed Susan* **

TRANSITION SLOPE / GRASSLAND
Elevation range: > +3.25 NAVD 88

photo: John Clare

scale: 1/3
specimen source: U.S. National Herbarium, Smithsonian Institution

12

6

Salicornia subterminalis Glasswort

TRANSITION SLOPE
Elevation range: > +3.25 NAVD 88

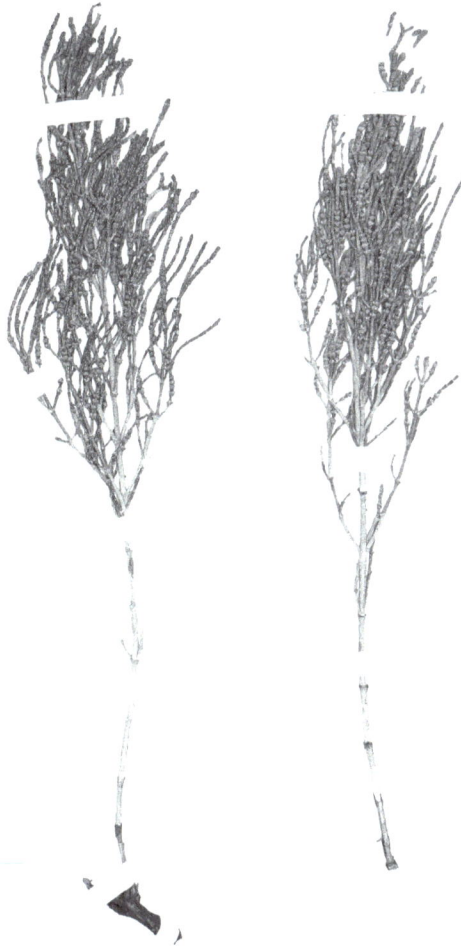

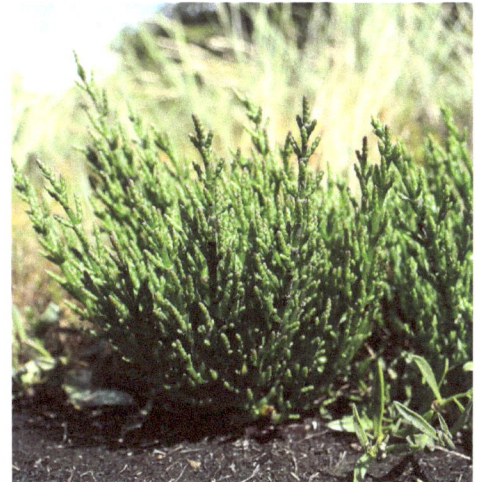

photo: Marco Schmidt, Wikipedia

scale: 1/3
specimen source: Herbarium of U.S. Department of Agriculture

18"

12"

6"

Solidago sempervirens Seaside Goldenrod* **

TRANSITION SLOPE / DUNE / GRASSLAND
Elevation range: > +3.25 NAVD 88

photo: Bill Hubick

scale: 1/3
specimen source: Herbier Museum Paris

Vernonia noveboracensis Ironweed* **

TRANSITION SLOPE / GRASSLAND
Elevation range: > +3.25 NAVD 88

photo: Jim Allison

scale: 1/3
specimen source: Tall Timbers Research Station

DUNE
elevation range: approx. +5 to +16 NAVD 88

Ammophila breviligulata	American Beach Grass* **
Myrica pensylvanica	Bayberry* **
Prunus maritima	Beach Plum* **
Rosa carolina	Pasture Rose**
Solidago sempervirens	Seaside Goldenrod* **

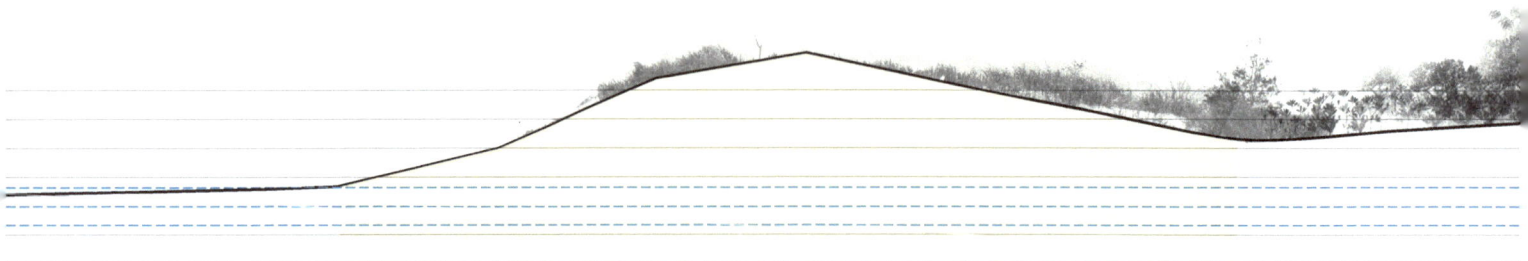

* used in restoration projects by the US Army Corps of Engineers

** recommended native plant by Natural Resources Group

Ammophila breviligulata   American Beach Grass* **

DUNE
Elevation range: approx. +5 to +16 NAVD 88

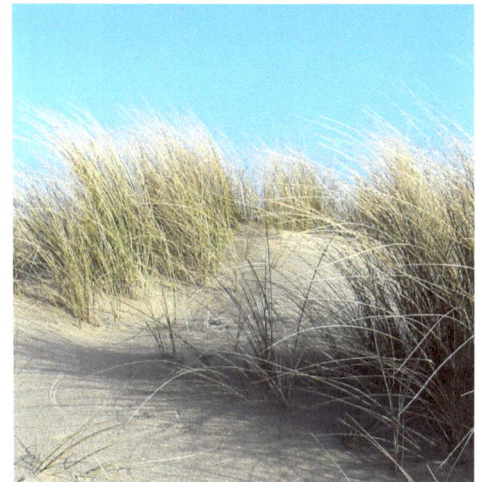

scale: 1/3
specimen source The Gray Herbarium

Myrica pensylvanica   Bayberry* **

DUNE / UPLAND SHRUB
Elevation range: approx. +5 to +16 NAVD 88

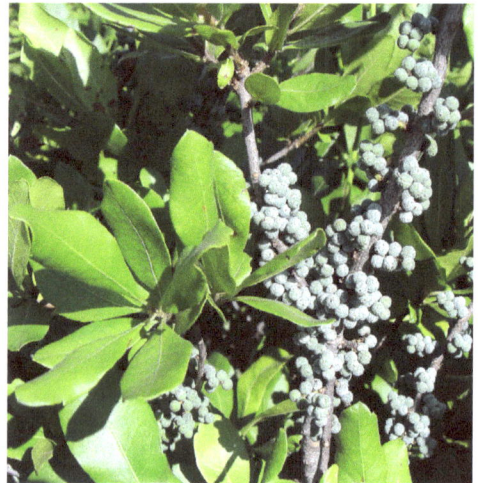

photo D. Cameron

scale: 1/3
specimen source: Tall Timbers Research Station

12'

Prunus maritima   Beach Plum* **

DUNE / UPLAND SHRUB
Elevation range: approx. +5 to +16 NAVD 88

6'

photo: ovsla.com

scale: 1/3
specimen source: Emily DeCamp Herbarium

Rosa carolina   Pasture Rose**

DUNE
Elevation range: approx. +5 to +16 NAVD 88

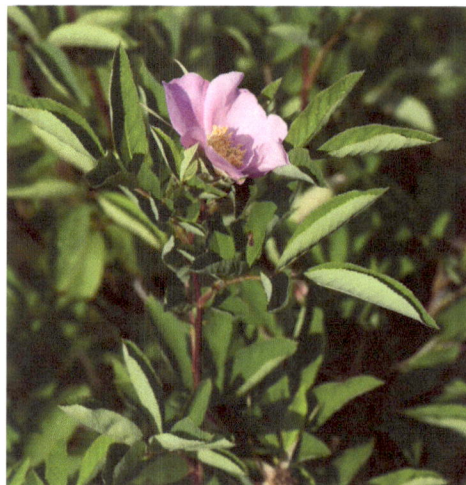

photo: florafinder.com

Solidago sempervirens   Seaside Goldenrod* **

TRANSITION SLOPE / DUNE / GRASSLAND
Elevation range: > +3.25 NAVD 88

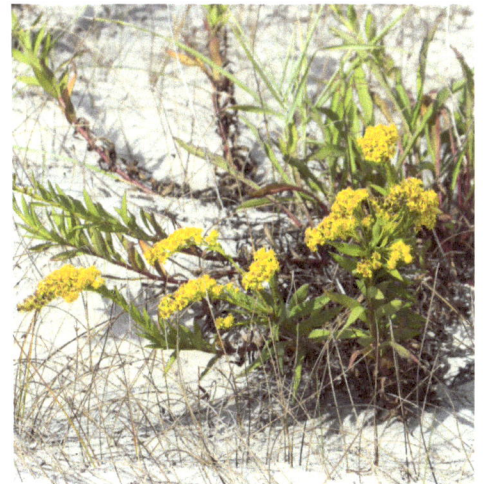

photo Bill Hubick

scale : 1/3
specimen source : Herbier Museum Paris

GRASSLAND
elevation range: varies (> +6 NAVD 88)

Andropogon virginicus	Broomsedge Bluestem* **
Apocynum cannabinum	Indian Hemp*
Asclepias syriaca	Milkweed* **
Asclepias tuberosa	Butterfly Milkweed* **
Aster laevis	Smooth Aster*
Avena sativa	Common Oat*
Carex pensylvanica	Pennsylvania Sedge* **
Deschampsia flexuosa	Wavy Hairgrass*
Eupatorium fistulosum	Joe Pye Weed* **
Eupatorium hyssopifolium	Hyssop-Leaved Thoroughwort*
Eupatorim maculatum	Spotted Joe Pye Weed* **
Monarda fistulosa	Wild Bergamot* **
Panicum virgatum	Switchgrass* **
Rudbeckia hirta	Black-Eyed Susan* **
Schizachyrium scoparium	Little Bluestem* **
Solidago sempervirens	Seaside Goldenrod* **
Vernonia noveboracensis	Ironweed* **

* used in restoration projects by the US Army Corps of Engineers

** recommended native plant by Natural Resources Group

Andropogon virginicus   Broomsedge Bluestem* **

GRASSLAND
Elevation range: varies (> +6 NAVD 88)

12

6

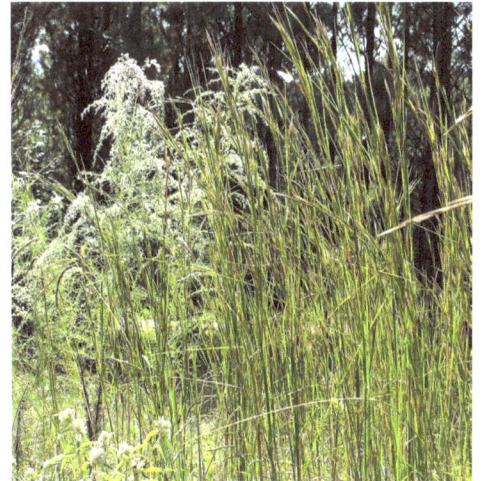

photo: galleryhip.com

scale: 1/3
specimen source: Naturhistorisches Museum Wien Botanische Abteilung

Apocynum cannabinum   Indian Hemp*

TRANSITION SLOPE / GRASSLAND
Elevation range: > +3.25 NAVD 88

photo: Russ Kleinman, Bill Norris, Kelly Kindscher

scale: 1/3
specimen source United States National Herbarium, Smithsonian Institution

12'

6'

Asclepias syriaca   Milkweed* **

TRANSITION SLOPE / GRASSLAND
Elevation range: > +3.25 NAVD 88

photo: Stefan Lefnaer, Wikipedia

scale: 1/3
specimen sources: Linnean Society of London Herbarium / New England Botanical Club

12"

6"

Asclepias tuberosa   Butterfly Milkweed* **

TRANSITION SLOPE / GRASSLAND
Elevation range: > +3.25 NAVD 88

photo: Rus Kleinman, Karen Blisard

scale: 1/3
specimen source: Herbarium Desert Botanical Garden

Aster laevis   Smooth Aster*

TRANSITION SLOPE / GRASSLAND
Elevation range: > +3.25 NAVD 88

photo: galleryhip.com

scale: 1/3
specimen source: Herbarium of the University of Washington

scale: 1/3
specimen source: Herbarium of the University of Tennessee

Avena sativa   Common Oat*

GRASSLAND
Elevation range: varies (> +6 NAVD 88)

photo: Rasbak, Wikimedia Commons

Carex pensylvanica Pennsylvania Sedge* **

TRANSITION SLOPE / GRASSLAND
Elevation range: > +3.25 NAVD 88

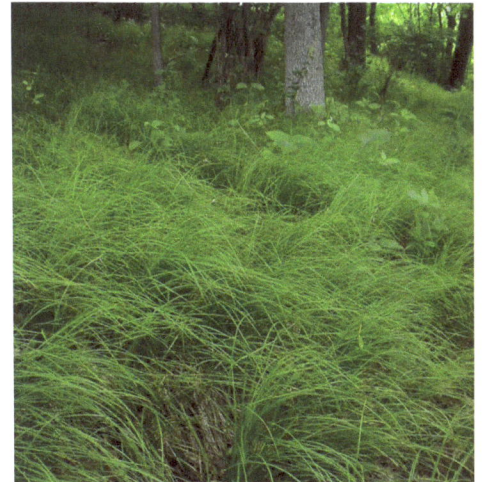

photo: nativeplant.com

scale: 1/3
specimen source: Academy of Natural Sciences, Philadelphia

12

6

Deschampsia flexuosa   Wavy Hairgrass*

GRASSLAND
Elevation range: varies (> +6 NAVD 88)

photo: cruydthoeck.nl

scale: 1/3
specimen source: The Natural History Museum, London

Eupatorium fistulosum   Joe Pye Weed* **

TRANSITION SLOPE / GRASSLAND
Elevation range: > +3.25 NAVD 88

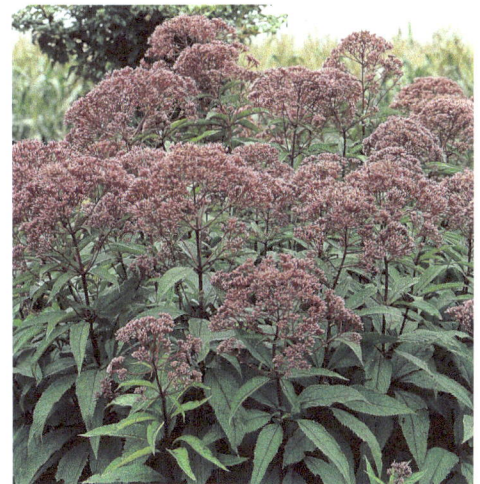

photo: Centre de Jardin Brossard

scale: 1/3
specimen source: Carnegie Museum of Natural History Herbarium

12"

6"

Eupatorium hyssopifolium   Hyssop-Leaved Thoroughwort* **

TRANSITION SLOPE / GRASSLAND
Elevation range: > +3.25 NAVD 88

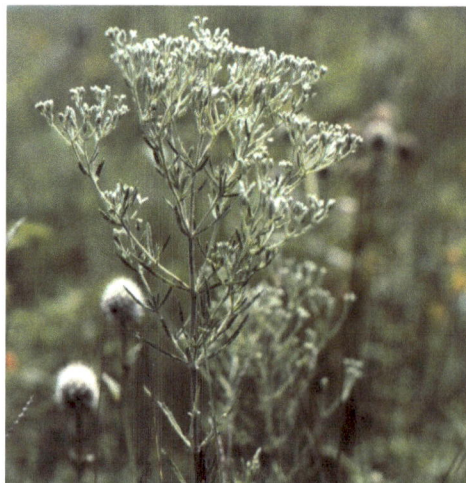

photo: Larry Allain, USDA NRCS PLANTS

scale: 1/3
specimen source: Natural History Museum

Eutrochium maculatum   Spotted Joe Pye Weed* **

TRANSITION SLOPE / GRASSLAND
Elevation range: > +3.25 NAVD 88

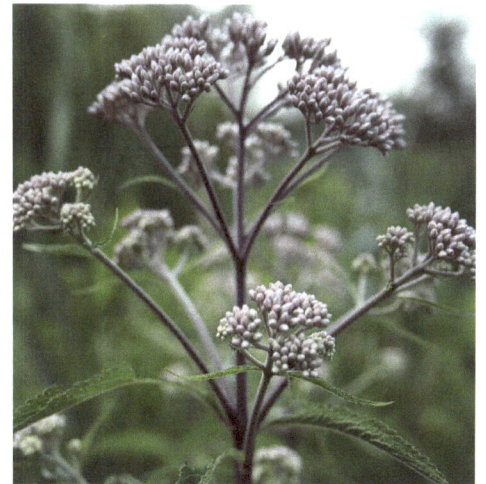

photo: Cody Hough, Wikimedia Commons

scale: 1/3
specimen source: Academy of Natural Sciences

12

6"

Monarda fistulosa   Wild Bergamot* **

TRANSITION SLOPE / GRASSLAND
Elevation range: > +3.25 NAVD 88

photo: Jacob Cline

scale: 1/3
specimen source: Herbarium of the University of West Alabama

12

Panicum virgatum   Switchgrass* **

TRANSITION SLOPE / GRASSLAND
Elevation range: > +3.25 NAVD 88

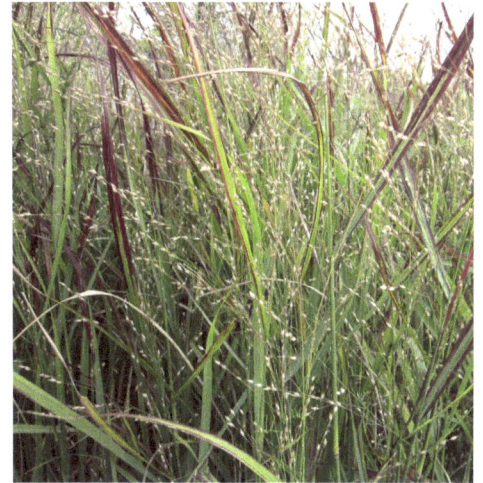

photo: Rose Kennedy Greenway

scale: 1/3
specimen source: U.S. National Herbarium, Smithsonian Institution

12

6

Rudbeckia hirta   Black-Eyed Susan* **

TRANSITION SLOPE / GRASSLAND
Elevation range: > +3.25 NAVD 88

photo: John Clare

scale: 1/3
specimen source: U.S. National Herbarium, Smithsonian Institution

Schizachyrium scoparium   Little Bluestem* **

GRASSLAND
Elevation range: varies (> +6 NAVD 88)

photo: rainbowbeachdunes.wordpress.com

scale: 1/3
specimen source: Missouri Botanical Garden

12"

6"

Solidago sempervirens   Seaside Goldenrod* **

TRANSITION SLOPE / DUNE / GRASSLAND
Elevation range: > +3.25 NAVD 88

photo: Bill Hubick

scale: 1/3
specimen source Herbier Museum Paris

Vernonia noveboracensis   Ironweed* **

TRANSITION SLOPE / GRASSLAND
Elevation range: > +3.25 NAVD 88

photo: Jim Allison

scale: 1/3
specimen source: Tall Timbers Research Station

UPLAND PERENNIAL / GROUND COVER
elevation range: > +4' NAVD 88

Artemisia stelleriana	Silver Brocade
Baccharis halimifolia	Sea-myrtle**
Cakile edentula	American Searocket
Cirsium horridulum	Yellow Thistle
Hieracium venosum	Rattlesnake Weed
Hudsonia tomentosa	Sand Heather
Iva frutescens linnaeus	Marsh Elder*
Lathyrus japonicus	Sea Pea
Parthenocissus quinquefolia	Virginia Creeper
Smilacina stellata	Star-flowered Solomon's Seal
Toxicodendron radicans	Poison Ivy*

* used in restoration projects by the US Army Corps of Engineers

** recommended native plant by Natural Resources Group

Artemisia stelleriana   Silver Brocade

UPLAND PERENNIAL / GROUND COVER
Elevation range: > +4' NAVD 88

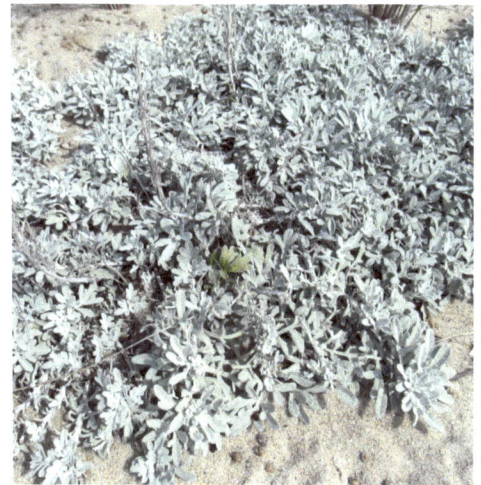

photo: John Phelan, Wikimedia Commons

scale: 1/3
specimen source: University of British Columbia Herbarium

Baccharis halimifolia   Sea-myrtle**

UPLAND PERENNIAL / GROUND COVER
Elevation range: > +4' NAVD 88

photo: Loughmiller, Cambell and Lynn, The University of Texas at Austin

12

6

scale: 1/3
specimen source: The William and Lynda Steere Herbarium of the New York Botanical Garden

Cakile edentula Sea Rocket

UPLAND PERENNIAL / GROUND COVER
Elevation range: > +4' NAVD 88

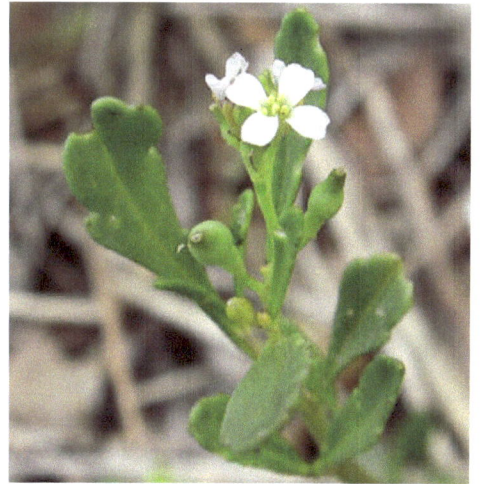

photo: Eleanor Saulys, Connecticut Botanical Society

scale: 1/3
specimen source: Rancho Santa Ana Botanic Garden

Cirsium horridulum   Yellow Thistle

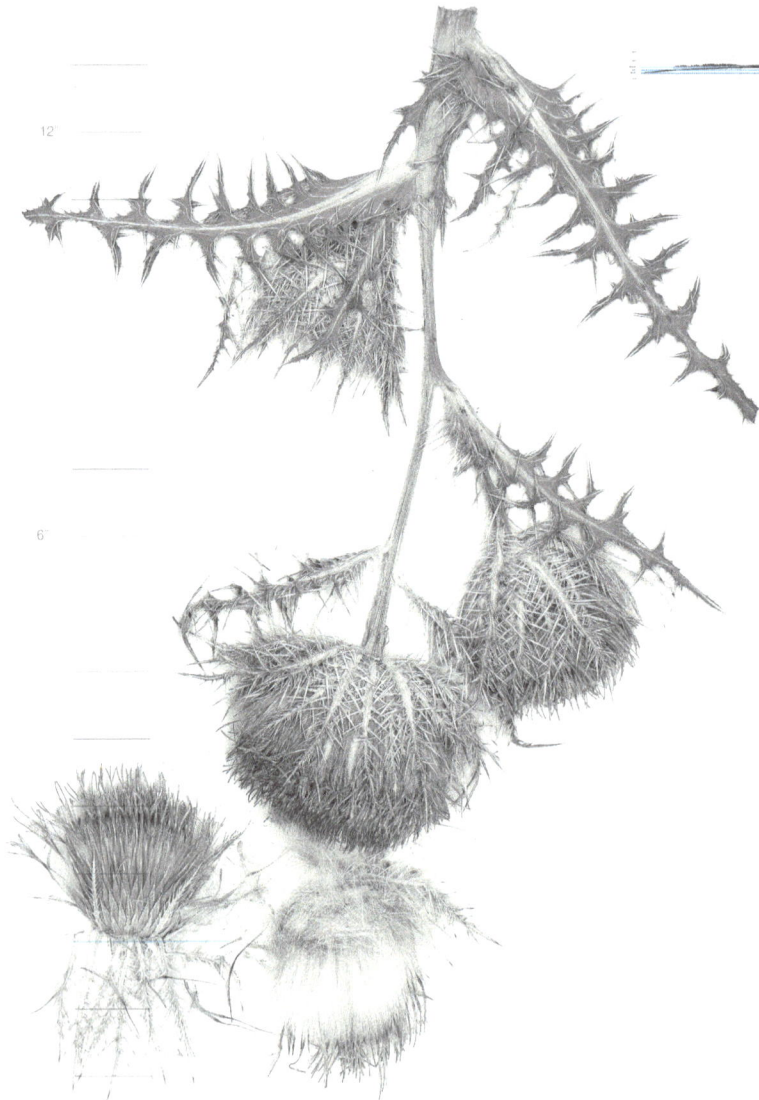

UPLAND PERENNIAL / GROUND COVER
Elevation range: > +4' NAVD 88

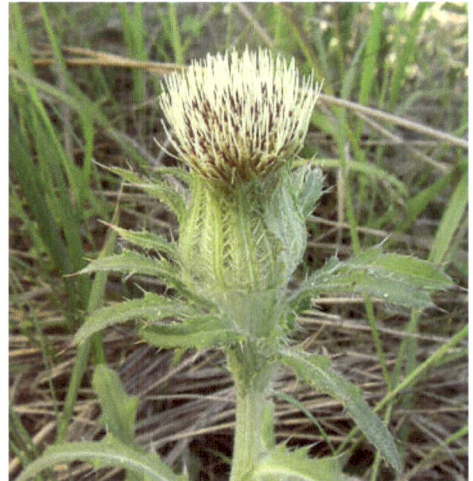

photo: Eleanor Saulys, Connecticut Botanical Society

scale: 1/3
specimen source   University of Texas Herbarium

Hieracium venosum   Rattlesnake Weed

UPLAND PERENNIAL / GROUND COVER
Elevation range: > +4' NAVD 88

photo: Jane Shelby Richardson, Duke University

scale: 1/3
specimen source: Linnean Society of London Herbarium

Hudsonia tomentosa   Sand Heather

UPLAND PERENNIAL / GROUND COVER
Elevation range: > +4' NAVD 88

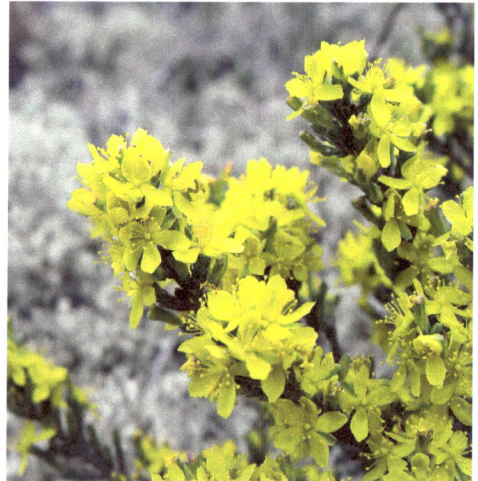

photo: Arthur Haines, New England Wildflower Society

scale: 1/3
specimen source: The Academy of Natural Sciences

12

6'

Iva frutescens linnaeus   Marsh Elder*

UPLAND PERENNIAL / GROUND COVER
Elevation range: > +4' NAVD 88

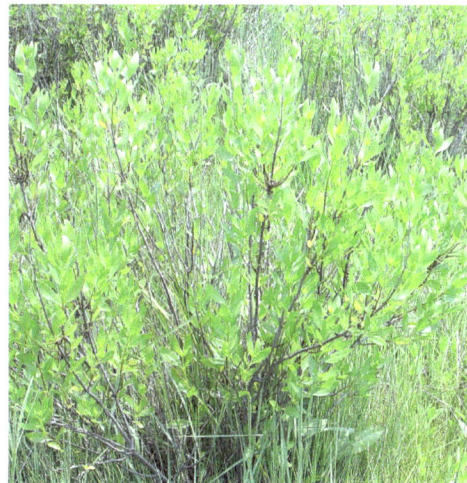

photo: Arthur Haines, New England Wildflower Society

scale: 1/3
specimen source: The Academy of Natural Sciences

Lathyrus japonicus   Sea Pea

UPLAND PERENNIAL / GROUND COVER
Elevation range: > +4' NAVD 88

photo: Peter M. Dziuk, Minnesota Wildflowers

scale: 1/3
specimen source: The Gray Herbarium, Harvard University

Parthenocissus quinquefolia Virginia Creeper

UPLAND PERENNIAL / GROUND COVER
Elevation range: > +4' NAVD 88

photo: SCR Jamaica Bay

scale: 1/3
specimen source: Herbarium of the Arnold Arboretum, Harvard University

Smilacina stellata   Star-flowered Solomon's Seal

UPLAND PERENNIAL / GROUND COVER
Elevation range: > +4' NAVD 88

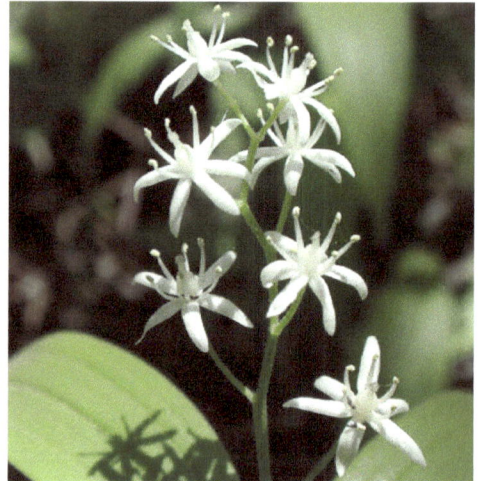

photo: Paul Slichter, science.halleyhosting.com

scale: 1/3
specimen source: The Gray Herbarium, Harvard University

Toxicodendron radicans   Poison Ivy*

UPLAND PERENNIAL / GROUND COVER
Elevation range: > +4' NAVD 88

photo: Wikipedia

scale: 1/3
specimen source: Troy University Herbarium

UPLAND SHRUB
elevation range: approx. > +6' NAVD 88

Amelanchier canadensis	Serviceberry* **
Aralia nudicaulis	Wild Sarsaparilla**
Arctostaphylos uva-ursi	Bearberry*
Myrica heterophylla	Swamp Bayberry
Myrica pensylvanica	Bayberry* **
Prunus maritima	Beach Plum* **
Rhus copallina	Winged Sumac* **
Rhus typhina	Staghorn Sumac**
Vaccinium corymbosum	High Bush Blueberry* **

* used in restoration projects by the US Army Corps of Engineers

** recommended native plant by Natural Resources Group

18

12'

6'

Amelanchier canadensis   Serviceberry* **

UPLAND SHRUB
Elevation range: approx. > +6' NAVD 88

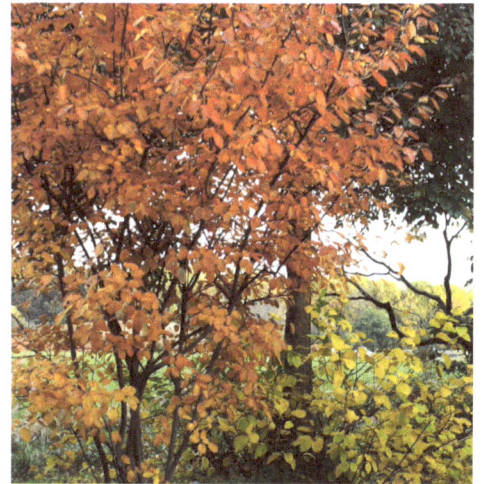

photo John Harrod. The Nature of Delaware

scale: 1/3
specimen source: Academy of Natural Sciences

Aralia nudicaulis   Wild Sarsaparilla**

UPLAND SHRUB
Elevation range: approx. > +6' NAVD 88

photo: Louis-M. Landry, UC Regents

scale: 1/3
specimen source: National Botanic Garden of Belgium

Arctostaphylos uva-ursi   Bearberry*

UPLAND SHRUB
Elevation range: approx. > +6' NAVD 88

photo: Wikimedia Commons

scale: 1/3
specimen source: United States National Herbarium, Smithsonian Institution

Myrica heterophylla   Swamp Bayberry

UPLAND SHRUB
Elevation range: approx. > +6' NAVD 88

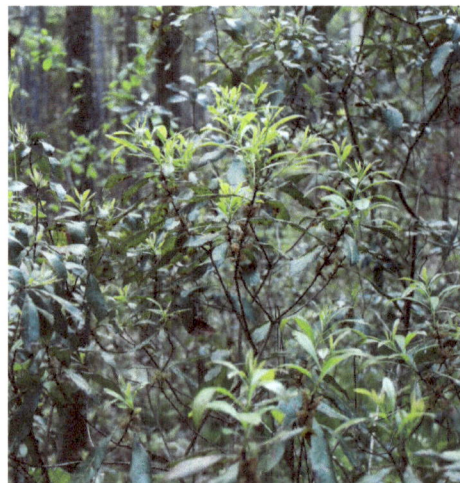

12

6'

photo: src.sfasu.edu

scale: 1/3
specimen source: Herbarium of Northeast Louisiana University

12

6

Myrica pensylvanica Bayberry* **

DUNE / UPLAND SHRUB
Elevation range: approx. +5 to +16 NAVD 88

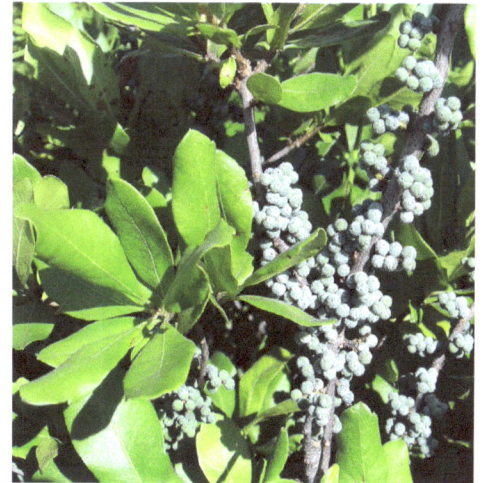

photo D. Cameron

scale: 1/3
specimen source: Tall Timbers Research Station

Prunus maritima   Beach Plum* **

DUNE / UPLAND SHRUB
Elevation range: approx. +5 to +16 NAVD 88

12"

6"

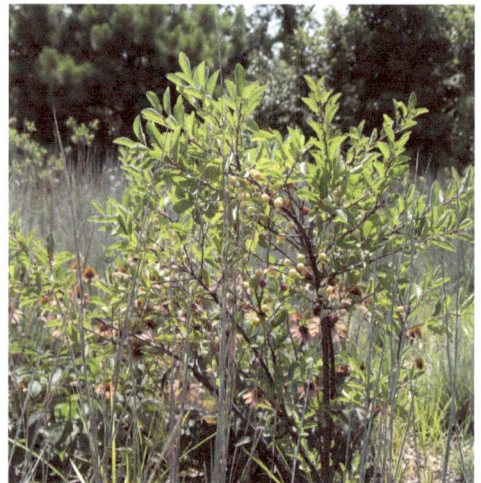

photo: ovsla.com

scale: 1/3
specimen source: Emily DeCamp Herbarium

12

6

Rhus copallina   Winged Sumac* **

UPLAND SHRUB
Elevation range: approx. > +6' NAVD 88

scale: 1/3
specimen source Linnean Society of London Herbarium

Rhus typhina   Staghorn Sumac**

UPLAND SHRUB
Elevation range: approx. > +6' NAVD 88

photo: Jean Gregory Evans

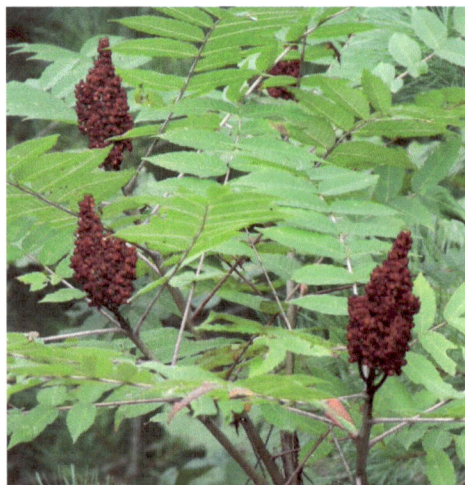

scale: 1/3
specimen source: Linnean Society of London Herbarium

Vaccinium corymbosum   High Bush Blueberry* **

UPLAND SHRUB
Elevation range: approx. > +6' NAVD 88

photo: vfthomas.com

scale: 1/3
specimen source: Academy of Natural Sciences

RIDGELINE

elevation range: varies, typical +12' to +17' NAVD 88

Pinus rigida   Pitch Pine* **

* used in restoration projects by the US Army Corps of Engineers

** recommended native plant by Natural Resources Group

18

Pinus rigida   Pitch Pine* **

RIDGELINE
Elevation range: +varies, typical +12' to +17' NAVD 88

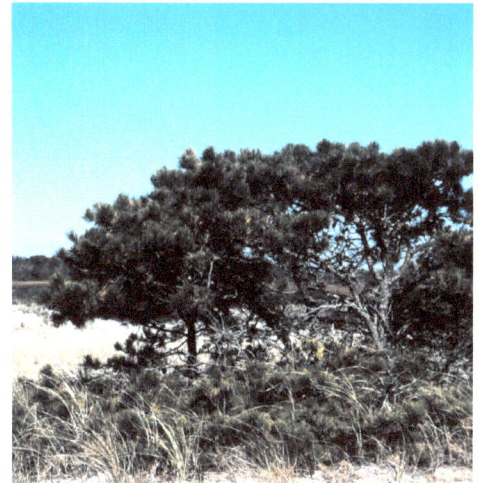

12

6'

photo: Wikipedia, public domain

scale: 1/3
specimen source Herbarium of the University of North Carolina

MARITIME FOREST

elevation range: ~ > +8' NAVD 88 to ridgeline

Acer rubrum	Red Maple**
Betula populifolia	Grey Birch* **
Celtis occidentalis	Hackberry* **
Ilex opaca	American Holly* **
Magnolia virginiana	Sweetbay Magnolia
Nyssa sylvatica	Black Tupelo**
Populus deltoides	Cottonwood*
Prunus serotina	Black Cherry* **
Quercus stellata	Post Oak
Quercus velutina	Black Oak* **
Salix pentandra	Bay Willow*
Sassafras albidum	Sassafras

* used in restoration projects by the US Army Corps of Engineers

** recommended native plant by Natural Resources Group

Acer rubrum   Red Maple**

MARITIME FOREST
Elevation range: ~ > +8' NAVD 88 to ridgeline

12

6

photo: South African National Biodiversity Institute, National Herbarium, Pretoria

scale: 1/3
specimen source: U.S. National Herbarium, Smithsonian Institution

Betula populifolia   Grey Birch* **

MARITIME FOREST
Elevation range: ~ > +8' NAVD 88 to ridgeline

12'

6'

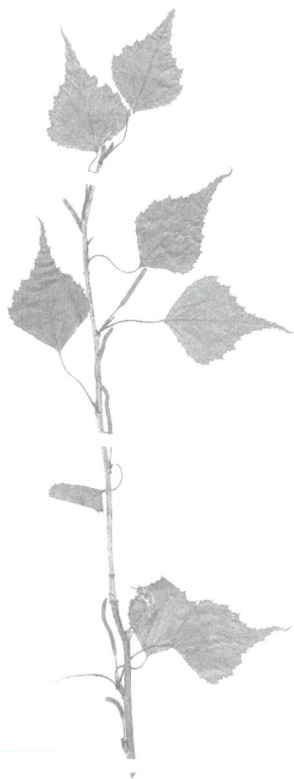

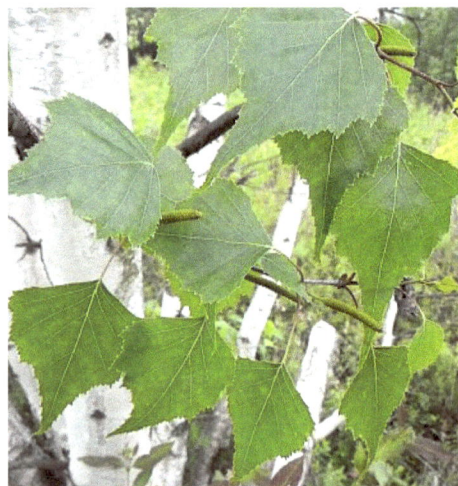

photo: www.illinoiswildflowers.info

scale: 1/3
specimen source: The Academy of Natural Sciences

12

6"

Celtis occidentalis   Hackberry* **

MARITIME FOREST
Elevation range: ~ > +8' NAVD 88 to ridgeline

photo Will Cook, www.carolinanature.com

scale: 1/3
specimen source: Royal Botanic Gardens

Ilex opaca   American Holly* **

MARITIME FOREST
Elevation range: ~ > +8' NAVD 88 to ridgeline

12

6'

photo: Missouri Botanical Garden

scale: 1/3
specimen source: The Gray Herbarium, Harvard University

12

6

Magnolia virginiana   Sweetbay Magnolia

MARITIME FOREST
Elevation range: ~ > +8' NAVD 88 to ridgeline

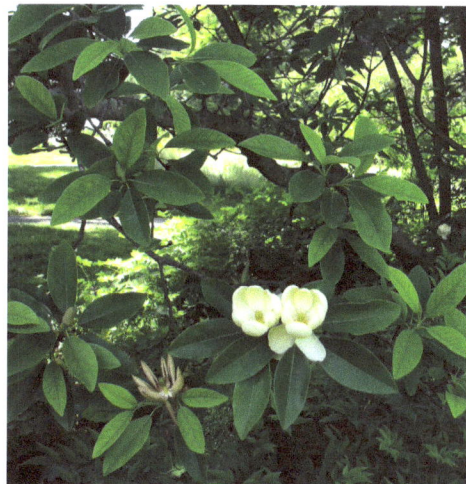

photo: Derek Ramsey, Wikimedia Creative Commons

scale: 1/3
specimen source: Royal Botanic Gardens, Kew

Nyssa sylvatica   Black Tupelo**

MARITIME FOREST
Elevation range: ~ > +8' NAVD 88 to ridgeline

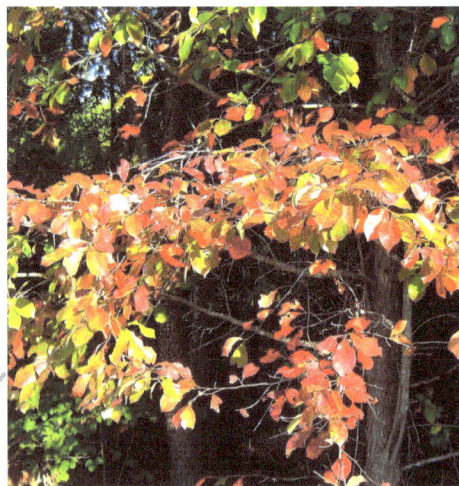

photo: flickrhivemind.net

scale: 1/3
specimen source: The Natural History Museum, London

Populus deltoides   Cottonwood*

MARITIME FOREST
Elevation range: ~ > +8' NAVD 88 to ridgeline

12"

6"

photo Dave Powell, USDA

scale: 1/3
specimen source: Troy University Herbarium

Prunus serotina   Black Cherry* **

MARITIME FOREST
Elevation range: ~ > +8' NAVD 88 to ridgeline

photo: Dennis Profant

scale: 1/3
specimen source: Rancho Santa Ana Botanic Garden

Quercus stellata   Post Oak

MARITIME FOREST
Elevation range: ~ > +8' NAVD 88 to ridgeline

photo: Marlene Hahn

scale: 1/3
specimen source: University of Illinois Herbarium

Quercus velutina   Black Oak* **

MARITIME FOREST
Elevation range: ~ > +8' NAVD 88 to ridgeline

12"

6"

scale: 1/3
specimen source Royal Botanic Gardens, Kew

Salix pentandra   Bay Willow*

MARITIME FOREST
Elevation range: ~ > +8' NAVD 88 to ridgeline

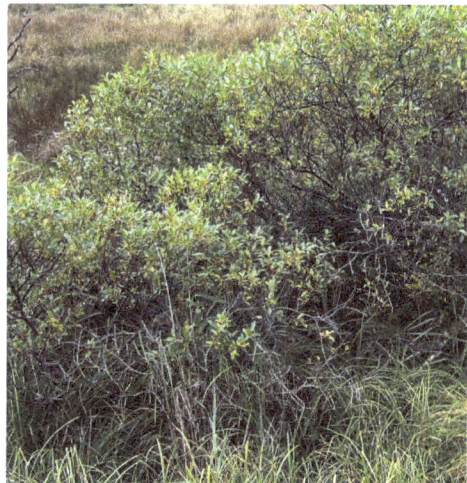

photo: Wikimedia Commons, MPF

scale: 1/3
specimen source: Universidad Nacional de Colombia

Sassafras albidum   Sassafras

MARITIME FOREST
Elevation range: ~ > +8' NAVD 88 to ridgeline

12

6'

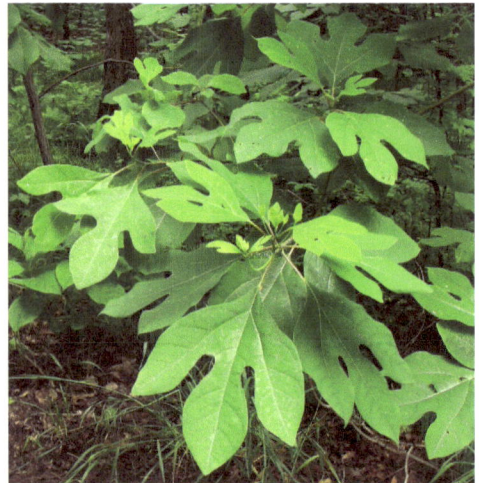

photo: perverdonk.com

scale: 1/3
specimen source   Herbarium of the University of North Carolina at Wilmington

www.ingramcontent.com/pod-product-compliance
Lightning Source LLC
Chambersburg PA
CBHW060813270326

41929CB00002B/22